NATIVE GUARD

Poetry by Natasha Trethewey

•

DOMESTIC WORK

BELLOCQ'S OPHELIA

NATIVE GUARD

NATIVE GUARD

Natasha Trethewey

A Mariner Book

HOUGHTON MIFFLIN COMPANY

Boston • New York

Library of Congress Cataloging-in-Publication Data
Trethewey, Natasha D., date.
Native guard / Natasha Trethewey.
p. cm.
Includes bibliographical references.
ISBN-13: 978-0-618-60463-0
ISBN-10: 0-618-60463-4
1. United States — History — Civil War, 1861–1865 —
Participation, African American — Poetry. 2. African
American soldiers — Poetry. 3. Racially mixed
people — Poetry. 4. Interracial marriage — Poetry.
5. Mississippi—Poetry. 6. Mothers — Poetry. I. Title.
PS3570.R433N38 2006
811'.6 — dc22   2005010649

ISBN-13: 978-0-618-87265-7 (pbk.)
ISBN-10: 0-618-87265-5 (pbk.)

Book design by Melissa Lotfy
Typeface is Miller Text

Printed in the United States of America

DOC 20 19 18 17 16 15 14
4500619782

CONTENTS

III

For my mother, in memory

Memory is a cemetery
I've visited once or twice, white
                        ubiquitous and the set-aside

Everywhere under foot . . .
                        —CHARLES WRIGHT

THEORIES OF TIME AND SPACE

You can get there from here, though
there's no going home.

Everywhere you go will be somewhere
you've never been. Try this:

head south on Mississippi 49, one-
by-one mile markers ticking off

another minute of your life. Follow this
to its natural conclusion — dead end

at the coast, the pier at Gulfport where
riggings of shrimp boats are loose stitches

in a sky threatening rain. Cross over
the man-made beach, 26 miles of sand

dumped on the mangrove swamp — buried
terrain of the past. Bring only

what you must carry — tome of memory,
its random blank pages. On the dock

where you board the boat for Ship Island,
someone will take your picture:

the photograph — who you were —
will be waiting when you return.

I

I'm going there to meet my mother
She said she'd meet me when I come
I'm only going over Jordan
I'm only going over home

— Traditional

THE SOUTHERN CRESCENT

1

In 1959 my mother is boarding a train.
She is barely sixteen, her one large grip
bulging with homemade dresses, whisper
of crinoline and lace, her name stitched
inside each one. She is leaving behind
the dirt roads of Mississippi, the film
of red dust around her ankles, the thin
whistle of wind through the floorboards
of the shotgun house, the very idea of home.

Ahead of her, days of travel, one town
after the next, and *California* — a word
she can't stop repeating. Over and over
she will practice meeting her father, imagine
how he must look, how different now
from the one photo she has of him. She will
look at it once more, pulling into the station
at Los Angeles, and then again and again
on the platform, no one like him in sight.

2

The year the old Crescent makes its last run,
my mother insists we ride it together.
We leave Gulfport late morning, heading east.
Years before, we rode together to meet
another man, my father, waiting for us
as our train derailed. I don't recall how

she must have held me, how her face sank
as she realized, again, the uncertainty
of it all — that trip, too, gone wrong. Today,

she is sure we can leave home, bound only
for whatever awaits us, the sun now
setting behind us, the rails humming
like anticipation, the train pulling us
toward the end of another day. I watch
each small town pass before my window
until the light goes, and the reflection
of my mother's face appears, clearer now
as evening comes on, dark and certain.

GENUS NARCISSUS

Faire daffadills, we weep to see
You haste away so soone.
— ROBERT HERRICK

The road I walked home from school
was dense with trees and shadow, creek-side,
and lit by yellow daffodils, early blossoms

bright against winter's last gray days.
I must have known they grew wild, thought
no harm in taking them. So I did —

gathering up as many as I could hold,
then presenting them, in a jar, to my mother.
She put them on the sill, and I sat nearby

watching light bend through the glass,
day easing into evening, proud of myself
for giving my mother some small thing.

Childish vanity. I must have seen in them
some measure of myself — the slender stems,
each blossom a head lifted up

toward praise, or bowed to meet its reflection.
Walking home those years ago, I knew nothing
of Narcissus or the daffodils' short spring —

how they'd dry like graveside flowers, rustling
when the wind blew — a whisper, treacherous,
from the sill. *Be taken with yourself,*

they said to me; *Die early*, to my mother.

GRAVEYARD BLUES

It rained the whole time we were laying her down;
Rained from church to grave when we put her down.
The suck of mud at our feet was a hollow sound.

When the preacher called out I held up my hand;
When he called for a witness I raised my hand —
Death stops the body's work, the soul's a journeyman.

The sun came out when I turned to walk away,
Glared down on me as I turned and walked away —
My back to my mother, leaving her where she lay.

The road going home was pocked with holes,
That home-going road's always full of holes;
Though we slow down, time's wheel still rolls.

I wander now among names of the dead:
My mother's name, stone pillow for my head.

WHAT THE BODY CAN SAY

Even in stone the gesture is unmistakable —
the man upright, though on his knees, spine

arched, head flung back, and, covering his eyes,
his fingers spread across his face. I think

grief, and since he's here, in the courtyard
of the divinity school, *what he might ask of God.*

How easy it is to read this body's language,
or those gestures we've come to know — the raised thumb

that is both a symbol of agreement and the request
for a ride, the two fingers held up that once meant

victory, then *peace.* But what was my mother saying
that day not long before her death — her face tilted up

at me, her mouth falling open, wordless, just as
we open our mouths in church to take in the wafer,

meaning *communion?* What matters is context —
the side of the road, or that my mother wanted

something I still can't name: what, kneeling,
my face behind my hands, I might ask of God.

PHOTOGRAPH: ICE STORM, 1971

Why the rough edge of beauty? Why
the tired face of a woman, suffering,
made luminous by the camera's eye?

Or the storm that drives us inside
for days, power lines down, food rotting
in the refrigerator, while outside

the landscape glistens beneath a glaze
of ice? Why remember anything
but the wonder of those few days,

the iced trees, each leaf in its glassy case?
The picture we took that first morning,
the front yard a beautiful, strange place —

why on the back has someone made a list
of our names, the date, the event: nothing
of what's inside — mother, stepfather's fist?

WHAT IS EVIDENCE

Not the fleeting bruises she'd cover
with makeup, a dark patch as if imprint
of a scope she'd pressed her eye too close to,
looking for a way out, nor the quiver
in the voice she'd steady, leaning
into a pot of bones on the stove. Not
the teeth she wore in place of her own, or
the official document — its seal
and smeared signature — fading already,
the edges wearing. Not the tiny marker
with its dates, her name, abstract as history.
Only the landscape of her body — splintered
clavicle, pierced temporal — her thin bones
settling a bit each day, the way all things do.

LETTER

At the post office, I dash a note to a friend,
tell her I've just moved in, gotten settled, that

I'm now rushing off on an errand — except
that I write *errant,* a slip between letters,

each with an upright backbone anchoring it
to the page. One has with it the fullness

of possibility, a shape almost like the O
my friend's mouth will make when she sees

my letter in her box; the other, a mark that crosses
like the flat line of your death, the symbol

over the church house door, the ashes on your forehead
some Wednesday I barely remember.

What was I saying? I had to cross the word out,
start again, explain what I know best

because of the way you left me: how suddenly
a simple errand, a letter — everything — can go wrong.

AFTER YOUR DEATH

First, I emptied the closets of your clothes,
threw out the bowl of fruit, bruised
from your touch, left empty the jars

you bought for preserves. The next morning,
birds rustled the fruit trees, and later
when I twisted a ripe fig loose from its stem,

I found it half eaten, the other side
already rotting, or — like another I plucked
and split open — being taken from the inside:

a swarm of insects hollowing it. I'm too late,
again, another space emptied by loss.
Tomorrow, the bowl I have yet to fill.

MYTH

I was asleep while you were dying.
It's as if you slipped through some rift, a hollow
I make between my slumber and my waking,

the Erebus I keep you in, still trying
not to let go. You'll be dead again tomorrow,
but in dreams you live. So I try taking

you back into morning. Sleep-heavy, turning,
my eyes open, I find you do not follow.
Again and again, this constant forsaking.

*

Again and again, this constant forsaking:
my eyes open, I find you do not follow.
You back into morning, sleep-heavy, turning.

But in dreams you live. So I try taking,
not to let go. You'll be dead again tomorrow.
The Erebus I keep you in — still, trying —

I make between my slumber and my waking.
It's as if you slipped through some rift, a hollow.
I was asleep while you were dying.

AT DUSK

At first I think she is calling a child,
my neighbor, leaning through her doorway
at dusk, street lamps just starting to hum
the backdrop of evening. Then I hear
the high-pitched wheedling we send out
to animals who know only sound, not
the meanings of our words — *here here* —
nor how they sometimes fall short.
In another yard, beyond my neighbor's
sight, the cat lifts her ears, turns first
toward the voice, then back
to the constellation of fireflies flickering
near her head. It's as if she can't decide
whether to leap over the low hedge,
the neat row of flowers, and bound
onto the porch, into the steady circle
of light, or stay where she is: luminous
possibility — all that would keep her
away from home — flitting before her.
I listen as my neighbor's voice trails off.
She's given up calling for now, left me
to imagine her inside the house waiting,
perhaps in a chair in front of the TV,
or walking around, doing small tasks;
left me to wonder that I too might lift
my voice, sure of someone out there,
send it over the lines stitching here
to there, certain the sounds I make
are enough to call someone home.

II

Everybody knows about Mississippi.

—NINA SIMONE

PILGRIMAGE

Vicksburg, Mississippi

Here, the Mississippi carved
    its mud-dark path, a graveyard

for skeletons of sunken riverboats.
    Here, the river changed its course,

turning away from the city
    as one turns, forgetting, from the past —

the abandoned bluffs, land sloping up
    above the river's bend — where now

the Yazoo fills the Mississippi's empty bed.
    Here, the dead stand up in stone, white

marble, on Confederate Avenue. I stand
    on ground once hollowed by a web of caves;

they must have seemed like catacombs,
    in 1863, to the woman sitting in her parlor,

candlelit, underground. I can see her
    listening to shells explode, writing herself

into history, asking *what is to become*
    of all the living things in this place?

This whole city is a grave. Every spring —
    Pilgrimage — the living come to mingle

with the dead, brush against their cold shoulders
in the long hallways, listen all night

to their silence and indifference, relive
their dying on the green battlefield.

At the museum, we marvel at their clothes —
preserved under glass — so much smaller

than our own, as if those who wore them
were only children. We sleep in their beds,

the old mansions hunkered on the bluffs, draped
in flowers — funereal — a blur

of petals against the river's gray.
The brochure in my room calls this

living history. The brass plate on the door reads
Prissy's Room. A window frames

the river's crawl toward the Gulf. In my dream,
the ghost of history lies down beside me,

rolls over, pins me beneath a heavy arm.

SCENES FROM A DOCUMENTARY
HISTORY OF MISSISSIPPI

1. King Cotton, 1907

From every corner of the photograph, flags wave down
the main street in Vicksburg. Stacked to form an arch,
the great bales of cotton rise up from the ground

like a giant swell, a wave of history flooding the town.
When Roosevelt arrives — a parade — the band will march,
and from every street corner, flags wave down.

Words on a banner, *Cotton, America's King,* have the sound
of progress. This is two years before the South's countermarch —
the great bolls of cotton, risen up from the ground,

infested with boll weevils — a plague, biblical, all around.
Now, negro children ride the bales, clothes stiff with starch.
From up high, in the photograph, they wave flags down

for the President who will walk through the arch, bound
for the future, his back to us. The children, on their perch —
those great bales of cotton rising up from the ground —

stare out at us. Cotton surrounds them, a swell, a great mound
bearing them up, back toward us. From the arch,
from every corner of the photograph, flags wave down,
and great bales of cotton rise up from the ground.

2. Glyph, Aberdeen 1913

The child's head droops as if in sleep.
Stripped to the waist, in profile, he's balanced
on the man's lap. The man, gaunt in his overalls,
cradles the child's thin arm — the sharp elbow, white
signature of skin and bone — pulls it forward
to show the deformity — the humped back, curve
of spine — punctuating the routine hardships
of their lives: how the child must follow him
into the fields, haunting the long hours
slumped beside a sack, his body asking
how much cotton? or in the kitchen, leaning
into the icebox, *how much food?* or
kneeling beside him at the church house,
why, Lord, why? They pose as if to say
Look, this is the outline of suffering:
the child shouldering it — a mound
like dirt heaped on a grave.

3. Flood

They have arrived on the back
of the swollen river, the barge
dividing it, their few belongings
clustered about their feet. Above them
the National Guard hunkers
on the levee; rifles tight in their fists,
they block the path to high ground.
One group of black refugees,

the caption tells us, *was ordered*
to sing their passage onto land,
like a chorus of prayer — their tongues
the tongues of dark bells. Here,
the camera finds them still. Posed
as if for a school-day portrait,
children lace fingers in their laps.
One boy gestures allegiance, right hand
over the heart's charged beating.

The great river all around, the barge
invisible beneath their feet, they fix
on what's before them: the opening
in the sight of a rifle; the camera's lens;
the muddy cleft between barge and dry land —
all of it aperture, the captured moment's
chasm in time. Here, in the angled light
of 1927, they are refugees from history:
the barge has brought them this far;
they are waiting to disembark.

4. You Are Late

The sun is high and the child's shadow,
almost fully beneath her, touches the sole
of her bare foot on concrete. Even though
it must be hot, she takes the step; her goal

to read is the subject of this shot — a book
in her hand, the library closed, the door
just out of reach. Stepping up, she must look
at the two signs, read them slowly once more.

The first one, in pale letters, barely shows
against the white background. Though she will read
Greenwood Public Library for Negroes,
the other, bold letters on slate, will lead

her away, out of the frame, a finger
pointing left. I want to call her, say *wait.*
But this is history: she can't linger.
She'll read the sign that I read: *You Are Late.*

NATIVE GUARD

If this war is to be forgotten, I ask in the name of all
things sacred what shall men remember?
— FREDERICK DOUGLASS

November 1862

Truth be told, I do not want to forget
anything of my former life: the landscape's
song of bondage — dirge in the river's throat
where it churns into the Gulf, wind in trees
choked with vines. I thought to carry with me
want of freedom though I had been freed,
remembrance not constant recollection.
Yes: I was born a slave, at harvest time,
in the Parish of Ascension; I've reached
thirty-three with history of one younger
inscribed upon my back. I now use ink
to keep record, a closed book, not the lure
of memory — flawed, changeful — that dulls the lash
for the master, sharpens it for the slave.

December 1862

For the slave, having a master sharpens
the bend into work, the way the sergeant
moves us now to perfect battalion drill,
dress parade. Still, we're called supply units —
not infantry — and so we dig trenches,
haul burdens for the army no less heavy
than before. I heard the colonel call it
nigger work. Half rations make our work
familiar still. We take those things we need
from the Confederates' abandoned homes:

salt, sugar, even this journal, near full
with someone else's words, overlapped now,
crosshatched beneath mine. On every page,
his story intersecting with my own.

January 1863

O how history intersects — my own
berth upon a ship called the *Northern Star*
and I'm delivered into a new life,
Fort Massachusetts: a great irony —
both path and destination of freedom
I'd not dared to travel. Here, now, I walk
ankle-deep in sand, fly-bitten, nearly
smothered by heat, and yet I can look out
upon the Gulf and see the surf breaking,
tossing the ships, the great gunboats bobbing
on the water. And are we not the same,
slaves in the hands of the master, destiny?
— night sky red with the promise of fortune,
dawn pink as new flesh: healing, unfettered.

January 1863

Today, dawn red as warning. Unfettered
supplies, stacked on the beach at our landing,
washed away in the storm that rose too fast,
caught us unprepared. Later, as we worked,
I joined in the low singing someone raised
to pace us, and felt a bond in labor
I had not known. It was then a dark man
removed his shirt, revealed the scars, crosshatched
like the lines in this journal, on his back.

It was he who remarked at how the ropes
cracked like whips on the sand, made us take note
of the wild dance of a tent loosed by wind.
We watched and learned. Like any shrewd master,
we know now to tie down what we will keep.

February 1863

We know it is our duty now to keep
white men as prisoners — rebel soldiers,
would-be masters. We're all bondsmen here, each
to the other. Freedom has gotten them
captivity. For us, a conscription
we have chosen — jailors to those who still
would have us slaves. They are cautious, dreading
the sight of us. Some neither read nor write,
are laid too low and have few words to send
but those I give them. Still, they are wary
of a negro writing, taking down letters.
X binds them to the page — a mute symbol
like the cross on a grave. I suspect they fear
I'll listen, put something else down in ink.

March 1863

I listen, put down in ink what I know
they labor to say between silences
too big for words: worry for beloveds —
My Dearest, how are you getting along —
what has become of their small plots of land —
did you harvest enough food to put by?
They long for the comfort of former lives —
I see you as you were, waving goodbye.

Some send photographs — a likeness in case
the body can't return. Others dictate
harsh facts of this war: *The hot air carries*
the stench of limbs, rotten in the bone pit.
Flies swarm — a black cloud. We hunger, grow weak.
When men die, we eat their share of hardtack.

April 1863

When men die, we eat their share of hardtack
trying not to recall their hollow sockets,
the worm-stitch of their cheeks. Today we buried
the last of our dead from Pascagoula,
and those who died retreating to our ship —
white sailors in blue firing upon us
as if we were the enemy. I'd thought
the fighting over, then watched a man fall
beside me, knees-first as in prayer, then
another, his arms outstretched as if borne
upon the cross. Smoke that rose from each gun
seemed a soul departing. The Colonel said:
an unfortunate incident; said:
their names shall deck the page of history.

June 1863

Some names shall deck the page of history
as it is written on stone. Some will not.
Yesterday, word came of colored troops, dead
on the battlefield at Port Hudson; how
General Banks was heard to say *I have*
no dead there, and left them, unclaimed. Last night,
I dreamt their eyes still open — dim, clouded

as the eyes of fish washed ashore, yet fixed —
staring back at me. Still, more come today
eager to enlist. Their bodies — haggard
faces, gaunt limbs — bring news of the mainland.
Starved, they suffer like our prisoners. Dying,
they plead for what we do not have to give.
Death makes equals of us all: a fair master.

August 1864

Dumas was a fair master to us all.
He taught me to read and write: I was a man-
servant, if not a man. At my work,
I studied natural things — all manner
of plants, birds I draw now in my book: wren,
willet, egret, loon. Tending the gardens,
I thought only to study live things, thought
never to know so much about the dead.
Now I tend Ship Island graves, mounds like dunes
that shift and disappear. I record names,
send home simple notes, not much more than how
and when — an official duty. I'm told
it's best to spare most detail, but I know
there are things which must be accounted for.

1865

These are things which must be accounted for:
slaughter under the white flag of surrender —
black massacre at Fort Pillow; our new name,
the Corps d'Afrique — words that take the *native*
from our claim; mossbacks and freedmen — exiles
in their own homeland; the diseased, the maimed,

every lost limb, and what remains: phantom
ache, memory haunting an empty sleeve;
the hog-eaten at Gettysburg, unmarked
in their graves; all the dead letters, unanswered;
untold stories of those that time will render
mute. Beneath battlefields, green again,
the dead molder — a scaffolding of bone
we tread upon, forgetting. Truth be told.

AGAIN, THE FIELDS

AFTER WINSLOW HOMER

the dead they lay long the lines like sheaves of Wheat I could have
walked on the boddes all most from one end too the other

No more muskets, the bone-drag
weariness of marching, the trampled
grass, soaked earth red as the wine

of sacrament. Now, the veteran
turns toward a new field, bright
as domes of the republic. Here,

he has shrugged off the past — his jacket
and canteen flung down in the corner.
At the center of the painting, he anchors

the trinity, joining earth and sky.
The wheat falls beneath his scythe —
a language of bounty — the swaths

like scripture on the field's open page.
Boundless, the wheat stretches beyond
the frame, as if toward a distant field —

the white canvas where sky and cotton
meet, where another veteran toils,
his hands the color of dark soil.

III

O magnet-South! O glistening perfumed South! my South!
O quick mettle, rich blood, impulse and love! good and evil!
  O all dear to me!
—WALT WHITMAN

PASTORAL

In the dream, I am with the Fugitive
Poets. We're gathered for a photograph.
Behind us, the skyline of Atlanta
hidden by the photographer's backdrop —
a lush pasture, green, full of soft-eyed cows
lowing, a chant that sounds like *no, no. Yes,*
I say to the glass of bourbon I'm offered.
We're lining up now — Robert Penn Warren,
his voice just audible above the drone
of bulldozers, telling us where to stand.
Say "race," the photographer croons. I'm in
blackface again when the flash freezes us.
My father's white, I tell them, *and rural.*
You don't hate the South? they ask. *You don't hate it?*

MISCEGENATION

In 1965 my parents broke two laws of Mississippi;
they went to Ohio to marry, returned to Mississippi.

They crossed the river into Cincinnati, a city whose name
begins with a sound like *sin*, the sound of wrong — *mis* in Mississippi.

A year later they moved to Canada, followed a route the same
as slaves, the train slicing the white glaze of winter, leaving Mississippi.

Faulkner's Joe Christmas was born in winter, like Jesus, given his name
for the day he was left at the orphanage, his race unknown in Mississippi.

My father was reading *War and Peace* when he gave me my name.
I was born near Easter, 1966, in Mississippi.

When I turned 33 my father said, *It's your Jesus year — you're the same
age he was when he died.* It was spring, the hills green in Mississippi.

I know more than Joe Christmas did. Natasha is a Russian name —
though I'm not; it means *Christmas child,* even in Mississippi.

MY MOTHER DREAMS ANOTHER COUNTRY

Already the words are changing. She is changing
    from *colored* to *negro, black* still years ahead.
This is 1966 — she is married to a white man —
    and there are more names for what grows inside her.
It is enough to worry about words like *mongrel*
    and the infertility of mules and *mulattoes*
while flipping through a book of baby names.
    She has come home to wait out the long months,
her room unchanged since she's been gone:
    dolls winking down from every shelf — all of them
white. Every day she is flanked by the rituals of superstition,
    and there is a name she will learn for this too:
maternal impression — the shape, like an unknown
    country, marking the back of the newborn's thigh.
For now, women tell her to clear her head, to steady her hands
    or she'll gray a lock of the child's hair wherever
she worries her own, imprint somewhere the outline
    of a thing she craves too much. They tell her
to stanch her cravings by eating dirt. All spring
    she has sat on her hands, her fingers numb. For a while
each day, she can't feel anything she touches: the arbor
    out back — the landscape's green tangle; the molehill
of her own swelling. Here — outside the city limits —
    cars speed by, clouds of red dust in their wake.
She breathes it in — *Mississippi* — then drifts toward sleep,
    thinking of someplace she's never been. Late,
Mississippi is a dark backdrop bearing down
    on the windows of her room. On the TV in the corner,
the station signs off, broadcasting its nightly salutation:
    the waving Stars and Stripes, our national anthem.

SOUTHERN HISTORY

Before the war, they were happy, he said,
quoting our textbook. (This was senior-year

history class.) *The slaves were clothed, fed,
and better off under a master's care.*

I watched the words blur on the page. No one
raised a hand, disagreed. Not even me.

It was late; we still had Reconstruction
to cover before the test, and — luckily —

three hours of watching *Gone with the Wind.*
History, the teacher said, *of the old South —*

a true account of how things were back then.
On screen a slave stood big as life: big mouth,

bucked eyes, our textbook's grinning proof — a lie
my teacher guarded. Silent, so did I.

BLOND

Certainly it was possible — somewhere
in my parents' genes the recessive traits
that might have given me a different look:
not attached earlobes or my father's green eyes,
but another hair color — gentleman-preferred,
have-more-fun blond. And with my skin color,
like a good tan — an even mix of my parents' —
I could have passed for white.

When on Christmas day I woke to find
a blond wig, a pink sequined tutu,
and a blond ballerina doll, nearly tall as me,
I didn't know to ask, nor that it mattered,
if there'd been a brown version. This was years before
my grandmother nestled the dark baby
into our crèche, years before I'd understand it
as primer for a Mississippi childhood.

Instead, I pranced around our living room
in a whirl of possibility, my parents looking on
at their suddenly strange child. In the photograph
my mother took, my father — almost
out of the frame — looks on as Joseph must have
at the miraculous birth: I'm in the foreground —
my blond wig a shining halo, a newborn likeness
to the child that chance, the long odds,
might have brought.

SOUTHERN GOTHIC

I have lain down into 1970, into the bed
my parents will share for only a few more years.
Early evening, they have not yet turned from each other
in sleep, their bodies curved — parentheses
framing the separate lives they'll wake to. Dreaming,
I am again the child with too many questions —
the endless *why* and *why* and *why*
my mother cannot answer, her mouth closed, a gesture
toward her future: cold lips stitched shut.
The lines in my young father's face deepen
toward an expression of grief. I have come home
from the schoolyard with the words that shadow us
in this small Southern town — *peckerwood* and *nigger
lover, half-breed* and *zebra* — words that take shape
outside us. We're huddled on the tiny island of bed, quiet
in the language of blood: the house, unsteady
on its cinderblock haunches, sinking deeper
into the muck of ancestry. Oil lamps flicker
around us — our shadows, dark glyphs on the wall,
bigger and stranger than we are.

INCIDENT

We tell the story every year —
how we peered from the windows, shades drawn —
though nothing really happened,
the charred grass now green again.

We peered from the windows, shades drawn,
at the cross trussed like a Christmas tree,
the charred grass still green. Then
we darkened our rooms, lit the hurricane lamps.

At the cross trussed like a Christmas tree,
a few men gathered, white as angels in their gowns.
We darkened our rooms and lit hurricane lamps,
the wicks trembling in their fonts of oil.

It seemed the angels had gathered, white men in their gowns.
When they were done, they left quietly. No one came.
The wicks trembled all night in their fonts of oil;
by morning the flames had all dimmed.

When they were done, the men left quietly. No one came.
Nothing really happened.
By morning all the flames had dimmed.
We tell the story every year.

PROVIDENCE

What's left is footage: the hours before
    Camille, 1969 — hurricane
        parties, palm trees leaning
in the wind,
    fronds blown back,

a woman's hair. Then after:
    the vacant lots,
    boats washed ashore, a swamp

where graves had been. I recall

how we huddled all night in our small house,
    moving between rooms,
        emptying pots filled with rain.

The next day, our house —
    on its cinderblocks — seemed to float

    in the flooded yard: no foundation

beneath us, nothing I could see
        tying us   to the land.
        In the water, our reflection
            trembled,
disappeared
when I bent to touch it.

MONUMENT

Today the ants are busy
    beside my front steps, weaving
in and out of the hill they're building.
    I watch them emerge and —

like everything I've forgotten — disappear
    into the subterranean — a world
made by displacement. In the cemetery
    last June, I circled, lost —

weeds and grass grown up all around —
    the landscape blurred and waving.
At my mother's grave, ants streamed in
    and out like arteries, a tiny hill rising

above her untended plot. Bit by bit,
    red dirt piled up, spread
like a rash on the grass; I watched a long time
    the ants' determined work,

how they brought up soil
    of which she will be part,
and piled it before me. Believe me when I say
    I've tried not to begrudge them

their industry, this reminder of what
    I haven't done. Even now,
the mound is a blister on my heart,
    a red and humming swarm.

ELEGY FOR THE NATIVE GUARDS

> *Now that the salt of their blood*
> *Stiffens the saltier oblivion of the sea . . .*
> —ALLEN TATE

We leave Gulfport at noon; gulls overhead
trailing the boat — streamers, noisy fanfare —
all the way to Ship Island. What we see
first is the fort, its roof of grass, a lee —
half reminder of the men who served there —
a weathered monument to some of the dead.

Inside we follow the ranger, hurried
though we are to get to the beach. He tells
of graves lost in the Gulf, the island split
in half when Hurricane Camille hit,
shows us casemates, cannons, the store that sells
souvenirs, tokens of history long buried.

The Daughters of the Confederacy
has placed a plaque here, at the fort's entrance —
each Confederate soldier's name raised hard
in bronze; no names carved for the Native Guards —
2nd Regiment, Union men, black phalanx.
What is monument to their legacy?

All the grave markers, all the crude headstones —
water-lost. Now fish dart among their bones,
and we listen for what the waves intone.
Only the fort remains, near forty feet high,
round, unfinished, half open to the sky,
the elements — wind, rain — God's deliberate eye.

SOUTH

Homo sapiens *is the only species*
to suffer psychological exile.
— E. O. WILSON

I returned to a stand of pines,
       bone-thin phalanx

flanking the roadside, tangle
       of understory — a dialectic of dark

and light — and magnolias blossoming
       like afterthought: each flower

a surrender, white flags draped
       among the branches. I returned

to land's end, the swath of coast
       clear cut and buried in sand:

mangrove, live oak, gulfweed
       razed and replaced by thin palms —

palmettos — symbols of victory
       or defiance, over and over

marking this vanquished land. I returned
       to a field of cotton, hallowed ground —

as slave legend goes — each boll
       holding the ghosts of generations:

those who measured their days
          by the heft of sacks and lengths

of rows, whose sweat flecked the cotton plants
          still sewn into our clothes.

I returned to a country battlefield
          where colored troops fought and died —

Port Hudson where their bodies swelled
          and blackened beneath the sun — unburied

until earth's green sheet pulled over them,
          unmarked by any headstones.

Where the roads, buildings, and monuments
          are named to honor the Confederacy,

where that old flag still hangs, I return
          to Mississippi, state that made a crime

of me — mulatto, half-breed — native
          in my native land, this place they'll bury me.

NOTES

EPIGRAPH (page ix)

From "Meditation on Form and Measure," in *Black Zodiac* by Charles Wright. New York: Farrar, Straus and Giroux, 1997.

"GENUS NARCISSUS"

Epigraph from "To Daffadills" by Robert Herrick (1591–1674).

EPIGRAPH (page 17)

From "Mississippi Goddamn," on *In Concert* by Nina Simone. Verve Records, 1964.

"PILGRIMAGE"

The question *what is to become of all the living things in this place?* is from *My Cave Life in Vicksburg* by Mary Webster Loughborough. New York, 1864.

"NATIVE GUARD"

Epigraph from "Address at the Grave of the Unknown Dead" by Frederick Douglass, Arlington, Virginia, May 30, 1871; quoted in *Race and Reunion: The Civil War in American Memory* by David Blight. Cambridge, Mass.: Belknap Press, 2001.

The first regiments of the Louisiana Native Guards were mustered into service in September, October, and November of 1862 — the 1st Regiment thus becoming the first officially sanctioned regiment of black soldiers in the Union Army, and the 2nd and 3rd made up of men who had been slaves only months before enlisting. During the war, the fort at Ship Island, Mississippi, called Fort Massachusetts, was maintained as a prison for Confederate soldiers — military convicts and prisoners of war — manned by the 2nd Regiment. Among the 2nd Regiment's officers was Francis E. Dumas — the son of a white Creole father and a mulatto mother — who had inherited slaves when his father died. Although Louisiana law prohibited him from manumitting these slaves, when he joined the Union Army, Dumas freed them and encouraged those men of age to join the Native Guards. (From *The Louisiana Native*

Guards: The Black Military Experience During the Civil War by James G. Hollandsworth. Baton Rouge: Louisiana State University Press, 1995.)

"NATIVE GUARD," *January 1863*

The Union ship *Northern Star* transported seven companies of the 2nd Louisiana Native Guards to Fort Massachusetts, Ship Island, on January 12, 1863. The lines ". . . I can look out/upon the Gulf and see the surf breaking,/tossing the ships, the great gunboats bobbing/on the water. And are we not the same,/slaves in the hands of the master, destiny?" are borrowed, in slightly different form, from *Thank God My Regiment an African One: The Civil War Diary of Colonel Nathan W. Daniels*, edited by C. P. Weaver. Baton Rouge: Louisiana State University Press, 1998.

"NATIVE GUARD," *April 1863*

On April 9, 1863, 180 black men and their officers went onto the mainland to meet Confederate troops near Pascagoula, Mississippi. After the skirmish, as the black troops were retreating (having been outnumbered by the Confederates), white Union troops on board the gunboat *Jackson* fired directly at them and not at oncoming Confederates. Several black soldiers were killed or wounded. The phrases *an unfortunate incident* and *their names shall deck the page of history* are also from *Thank God My Regiment an African One: The Civil War Diary of Colonel Nathan W. Daniels*.

"NATIVE GUARD," *June 1863*

During the battle of Port Hudson in May 1863, General Nathaniel P. Banks requested a truce to locate the wounded Union soldiers and bury the dead. His troops, however, ignored the area where the Native Guards had fought, leaving those men unclaimed. When Colonel Shelby, a Confederate officer, asked permission to bury the putrefying bodies in front of his lines, Banks refused, saying that he had no dead in that area. (From *The Louisiana Native Guards: The Black Military Experience During the Civil War*.)

"NATIVE GUARD," *1865*

In April 1864, Confederate troops attacked Fort Pillow, a Union garrison fifty miles north of Memphis. One correspondent, in a dispatch to the *Mobile Advertiser and Register*, reported that, after gaining control of the fort, the Confederates disregarded several individual attempts by the black troops to surrender, and "an indiscriminate slaughter followed" in which Colonel Nathan Bedford Forrest purportedly ordered the black troops "shot down like dogs." (From "The Fort Pillow Massacre: Assessing the Evidence," by John Cimprich, in *Black Soldiers in Blue: African-American Troops in the Civil War Era,* edited by John David Smith. Chapel Hill: University of North Carolina Press, 2002.)

"AGAIN, THE FIELDS"
After Winslow Homer's *The Veteran in a New Field,* 1865.
   Epigraph quoted by Bell Irvin Wiley and Horst D. Milhollen, in *They Who Fought Here.* New York: Macmillan, 1959.

"PASTORAL"
The final line, *You don't hate the South?* they ask. *You don't hate it?,* is borrowed, in slightly different form, from William Faulkner's character Quentin Compson at the end of *Absalom, Absalom!:* "I don't hate the south. I don't hate it."

"ELEGY FOR THE NATIVE GUARDS"
Epigraph from "Ode to the Confederate Dead" by Allen Tate, 1937.

"SOUTH"
Epigraph from *Consilience: The Unity of Knowledge* by E. O. Wilson. New York: Knopf, 1998.

Acknowledgments

Many thanks to the editors of the following journals in which these poems — sometimes in earlier versions — first appeared. *Agni:* "What the Body Can Say," "Letter." *The Atlanta Review:* "Blond," "Elegy for the Native Guards." *Callaloo:* "Native Guard," "What Is Evidence." *Crab Orchard Review:* "Again, the Fields," "Southern Gothic." *The Georgia Review:* "My Mother Dreams Another Country." *The Greensboro Review:* "Pastoral" (as "Southern Pastoral"), "Monument," "Southern History." *The Kenyon Review:* "Miscegenation." *Ms.:* "Photograph: Ice Storm, 1971." *New England Review:* "At Dusk," "After Your Death," "The Southern Crescent," "Genus Narcissus," "Myth." *PMS: Poem Memoir Story:* "Graveyard Blues." *Shenandoah:* "South." *Smartish Pace:* "Theories of Time and Space," "Providence." *Virginia Quarterly Review:* "Incident," "Scenes from a Documentary History of Mississippi," "Pilgrimage."

"After Your Death" also appeared in *The Best American Poetry 2003*, edited by Yusef Komunyakaa and David Lehman, published by Scribner, 2003.

My thanks as well to Emory University and the University Research Committee, the John Simon Guggenheim Memorial Foundation, and the Rockefeller Foundation Bellagio Study and Conference Center for generous fellowships and support that enabled me to complete this collection.